THE FUTURE OF

BITCOIN

AND RELATED

CRYPTOCURRENCIES

Disclosure

The author is a personal investor in a number of cryptocurrency markets. However, his personal investment perspective has no impact on contents herein.

Author's Note

This material covers bitcoin and related cryptocurrencies; those cryptocurrencies that haven't been developed any government.

The information contained in this book is for educational and general information purposes only. Any content herein shouldn't be considered advice or recommendations. You should consider legal, financial and taxation advice on how any of the information contained in this book relates to your personal circumstances.

While the author has made every effort to provide accurate Internet addresses at the time of publication, neither the author nor the publisher assumes any responsibility for errors, or for changes that occur after publication. Further, the publisher does not have any control over and does not assume any responsibility for author or third-party Web sites or their content.

"The future is already here – it's just not evenly distributed."

William Gibson

Contents

Acknowledgements

Thank you, GOD, for the gift of life, strength, and resilience to make this possible!
To the amazing and inspiring family and friends in my circle, thank you too. Life has been so much easier because of you.

The future of money is undoubtedly digital, but do bitcoin or related cryptocurrencies provide the ultimate deal?

LET'S START HERE

It all started at a snail's pace with the single idea of bitcoin, but has now exploded and given birth to thousands of other cryptocurrencies, with many more expected to surface in the days, months, and possibly years ahead. And in the process, many people have made a lot of money, whilst in equal reverse measure, others too have lost lots of money. It's a volatile, yet thrilling phenomenal that has opened doors of investment and trading opportunities to many people.

Well, for starters, a cryptocurrency would be suitably defined as money in soft or digital format, e-money or a digital medium of exchange. Bitcoin is the first cryptocurrency to be launched and began trading in early 2009. It was fundamentally designed to incorporate the age old cryptographic features with an objective of realizing a distributed, decentralized, safe and secure production and circulation.

Notably, unlike fiat money, the hard currency, whose system of production and circulation is prone to abuse, the system adopted in the production and circulation of bitcoin, through use of blockchain technology guarantees the accountability of each new coin introduced in the market - the relevant information is in public domain.

When Bitcoin was first launched, it was worth basically nothing, just a few pennies. Then in early 2011, it registered a price surge, moving from cents and gaining a solid dollar mark. Between 2011 and 2013, its price interchangeably swung up and down, eventually being valued at more $1000. And since then, its price has consistently risen and fallen (going as high as $17,900 in late 2017, and tanking downwards to $6200 in late February 2018).

An investment in bitcoin at an earlier stage saw a number of ordinary people turned into millionaires, and some millionaires and crypto-creators turned into billionaires. Simply imagine buying one bitcoin in 2013 for $1000, and selling it in December 2017 at $17000 - you would have made a supernormal profit there! It's the thirst for making such high profits that has continued to lure many into the crypto world – (in pursuit of making a big kill in the shortest time possible).

Nonetheless, the sad truth is, there is still insufficient relevant information on cryptocurrencies making it hard to foretell their true future potential. Consequently, the big question in the minds of many crypto enthusiasts has been; *"Do the current cryptocurrencies have a solid future?* When you read this material to its conclusion, you'll definitely unmask this mystery!

Information is power! Finding out the future of bitcoin and related cryptocurrencies is essential to anyone interested in investing in the coins. Interestingly, the beauty of this book lies in walking you through the invaluable hot, yet sensitive topics in the cryptocurrency world. Reading it to the end is therefore one invaluable investment you'll treasure forever!

And to kick us off, let's first establish whether bitcoin and related cryptocurrencies qualify as genuine digital currencies, or not?

DO BITCOIN AND RELATED CRYPTOCURRENCIES QUALIFY AS GENUINE DIGITAL CURRENCIES?

First, let's examine what it takes for an item to be treated as a currency, digital or fiat?

A currency, also widely known as money, is generally defined in terms of three key functions or services it provides: a *medium of exchange, store of value,* and *unit of account.* Particularly, the most essential function of money is that of a medium of exchange, meaning it can be used to make payments for goods and services.

In the world of economics, money is defined as *anything that is generally acceptable in exchange for goods and services.* Economists further note that there are three types of money: *fiat money, commodity money,* and *representative money.*

- **Fiat money:** These are the printed paper notes and the hard coins you see around.

- **Commodity money:** This is money that is in the form of some valuable commodity - such as gold.

- **Representative money:** Use of something to represent money. Did you know before fiat money was universally embraced, there are numerous places where people could pay for goods or services using commodities - such as tobacco or cereals such as maize and wheat?

Any acceptable currency anywhere in the world should posses the below key characteristics:

- Durability - It must be able to withstand physical wear and tear. In other words, the objects used in its making must guarantee its durability.

- Portability - People must be able to move around with money as they go about their businesses.

- Divisibility - It must be easily divided into smaller units / smaller denominations.

- Uniformity - Any two or more units of money must offer uniformity in form of value. Or to say, there must be uniformity in value in terms of what two units of money can buy.

- Limited supply - It must be made available only in limited quantities.

- Acceptability - Everyone should be able to accept money for exchange of goods or services.

From the above definitions, it's evident cryptocurrencies such as bitcoin do posses some characteristics similar to those of any acceptable currency; *limited supply, uniformity, divisibility, and portability*. Equally, just like any genuine currency, cryptocurrencies conveniently facilitate payments between involved parties and provide store of value. Interestingly, they perform these two roles even in situations where trust, or lack of trust, is a problem.

It's therefore without any doubt to conclude that, yes, bitcoin and related cryptocurrencies have what it takes to qualify as genuine digital currencies. However, it's shocking that many people still hold back from embracing the coins as ideal digital currencies. What could be their reason(s)?

WHY MANY STILL HOLD BACK FROM EMBRACING CRYPTOCURRENCIES

Well, allow me for the sake of deeper understanding of the subject to continue using bitcoin as a major representative of other cryptos. Although the mining and circulation processes of other cryptos may differ slightly or significantly from bitcoin's, it remains the pioneer cryptocurrency, therefore holding that precious key to what will eventually befall other cryptos –– whether they are universally embraced as genuine digital currencies, or not.

Did you know, although bitcoin has been around since late 2009, it only started drawing the attention of most people in 2013! And since then, many other cryptos have emerged. However, it's unbelievable, at the time of writing this book, cryptocurrencies are not yet universally treated as genuine digital currencies. Although they are backed by a few world governments such as Japan, their wallets together with value balances do not enjoy consumer protection.

Many believe that in their present format and what they term as *weird way of operation*, the coins don't qualify to be fully embraced as genuine digital currencies. Well, to be more specific, below are some of the reasons they front as a hindrance to embracing cryptocurrencies as true digital currencies:

- **Fewer user cases**

  Take bitcoin as an example. The original idea behind its *creation* was to get it utilized as a digital medium of exchange. However, due to the instability of its value (the volatility of its price), it's been tricky for most platforms to adopt it. Instead, many prefer trading it, thus shadowing its true potential.

  There is a lot of laxity with which other cryptos too are being adopted for their originally intended purpose. There are just a bunch of online stores that accept bitcoin and related cryptos. Weirdly, the growth potential of platforms accepting cryptos as medium of exchange isn't promising!

- **Lack of proper clarity on the values of cryptos**

Many are investing in cryptos out of speculation, while others are doing so out of fear of missing out, without exposure to relevant investment advice or information.

Cryptos such as bitcoin adopt a decentralized system of circulation, and are mined using complex mathematical formulae, thus making it hard to tell their actual values. Consequently, the vital assignment of estimating their true worth has largely been under the control of speculators! This has resultantly made many investors vulnerable, ending up defying the age-old invaluable investment principle *never invest in it if you don't understand it'*.

The crypto market is littered with many speculators who readily spread how valuable the coins are - all with a cheeky focus of wanting to enjoy momentary price influx just for their personal greed. Once they greedily fill up their wallets, they then embark on a viscous circle - *spreading negative news to get the prices to lower down, make purchases during the dip, and then embark on speculative tricks for realizing more profit.*

- **Extreme volatility**

The two core functions of money are: a store of value, and a trusted means of exchange. However, cryptocurrencies in their present form (at the time of writing this book) are good as a means of exchange, but perform worse as a store of value. Their values fluctuate too much. For example, today, one bitcoin might be worth a car, a candy the next day, a house the next moment, and then next to nothing in the next moment.

- **Operating in unregulated space**

One of the key challenges may people believe is a hindrance to embracing cryptos is the danger lurking in the unregulated space that the coins operate in. No government entity, insurance or financial institutions regulate the coins, thereby making any transaction-related-grievance redressal impossible. In the event you get ripped off in a crypto transaction, it's impossible to get the cryptos or your money back.

Equally, the cryptos are built on an open source, making it easy for any blockchain savvy person to copy and improve on their weaknesses *(speed, security, flexibility, size of blockchain's file, scalability etc)*. As a result, the market is poised to soon witness an influx of all sorts of cryptos - a fact already ongoing.

- **The issue of legality**

Although no country has at the time of writing this book declared bitcoin and related cryptos as a legal tender, no country has also declared them illegal, leaving crypto investors at the mercy of fellow investors. As at now, those who have invested in the coins have done so at their own risks. Many are investing in the coins with the hope that a number of old investors would keep on hanging on their coins as new investors come in day by day.

- **Fraudsters' arena**

The decentralization of cryptocurrencies such as bitcoin doesn't offer any meaningful redress to persons who might suddenly lose their coins. Still, there isn't any guarantee offered by crypto wallet providers against theft of cryptos from investors'' wallets, making hacking every crypto holder's nightmare.

Did you know anyone who knows your keys can anonymously spend all of your bitcoin? It's never easy telling whoever has hacked into your account, which is a major drawback on the pseudonymity granted to bitcoin holders.

Many fraudsters are taking advantage of lack of proper information regarding trading in cryptocurrencies and have thus launched all sorts of tricks to con innocent investors. While some promise to double or triple the initial investments over a short period of time, others offer fake buy/sell platforms, only to end up swindling investors.

- **Possible connection to illegal activities**

  Again, due to the pseudonymity of bitcoin's users, cybercriminals, terrorists and extortionists are finding it easy to mask their identities and addresses and utilize the coins to discreetly sponsor their ill motives - making it difficult for government authorities or relevant security institutions to establish and, or track down any of such illegal activities, thus limiting any useful redresses they might offer in case of an eventuality. Significantly, activities such as money laundering and financing of terrorist-related activities can be effectively supported unnoticed.

- **Capping production and circulation**

  Why would a cryptocurrency like bitcoin put a cap on the quantity of coins to be produced and put in circulation? The danger with such capping is that once that limit is realized, many investors will begin looking elsewhere for other coins without caps, thus lowering the true value of bitcoin, and possibly putting it in danger of collapse.

For bitcoin and related cryptos to be fully embraced by the masses, they deserve the backing of governments, relevant legislations, and adequate information on their true values and potential publicly availed. At the moment, they enjoy little support from various governments, limited to no legislations, and no known mechanism of telling their true values.

In the next chapter, let me take you in detail on the question of prices of cryptocurrencies.

THE QUESTION OF PRICES OF CRYPTOCURRENCIES

One of the most exciting areas of interest to many people has never been the potential of the coins, but their ideal prices. I asked four of my close friends about their thoughts on prices of cryptocurrencies, and below are the unbelievable feedback they shared with me:

- The First One: *Bitcoin and related altercoins are unique bubbles that will ultimately burst to unmask their real values. Right now, they are overvalued, uncontrolled and difficult to tell a valuable coin from a less valuable one.*

- The Second One: *Cryptocurrencies have already alerted the world on the need of a digital currency, and are right now at the mercy of various world governments' support. I am certain if the creators of coins fail to assign the right values to their creations, most world governments would step in to fill that void. But again, that would be detrimental to the gains already made by the coins as a price cap would most likely make many investors to look for other viable investment options.*

- The Third One: *The trading of cryptocurrencies has attracted a wider public interest, with many amateur investors leading the pack as early adopters. Where have the professional and institutional investors gone to? They are obviously shying away due to lack of clear measures that can be utilized to tell the exact value of any cryptocurrency.*

- The Fourth One: *What goes up must eventually come down. It's no secret that with time, the prices of bitcoin together with those of other cryptocurrencies will eventually come down. In fact, it's by coming down that they'll eventually crawl back to find their ideal prices.*

Possible causes of instability of prices of cryptocurrencies

You've most probably asked yourself why the prices of bitcoin and related cryptocurrencies have remained volatile ever since. Well, here below are some of the possible contributors:

- Very few people own large chunks of cryptocurrencies making it possible for them to manipulate the prices. Notably, there are reports that the initial upsurge in bitcoin prices was fueled by more demand but less supply; those with large chunks of the coin decided to hold on to them - only releasing smaller amounts, thus pushing the prices to balloon.

- The price of one coin would decline if there is more supply but less demand (if the number of coins availed for sale out-number the demand for that particular coin).

- Diversification - The price of highly valued coin such as bitcoin would be challenged if more people decided to invest more in other altercoins. Less demand for bitcoin and more demand for other altercoins would most definitely lower down the price of bitcoin.

- Lack of adequate information regarding the technology behind the creation of each coin, and its future potential makes many to rely on unreliable sources of information (largely speculation) when investing in cryptocurrencies, and thus end up buying and selling at speculative prices.

- Lack of regulation of the prices, leaving it to the upward and downward market forces of demand vs. supply.

Again, below is a quick summary of some of the other possible factors playing roles in fuelling an increase in prices of cryptocurrencies:

- Increased interest from the masses.
- Commitment and dedication of the coins' creators.
- Product improvement and success in experiments and implementations.
- Favorable regulatory support from governments.
- More endorsements by key public figures and personalities.
- Positive news coverage from various media outlets.

Also, below are some of the other factors fuelling the fall of cryptocurrency prices:

- Waning interest from the masses
- Failure in experiments and implementation
- Walking out of creators
- Unfavorable regulatory-related jitters from various world governments - including threats of potential bans
- Rebuke from key public figures and personalities
- Negative news coverage - cryptos are allergic to negative news and legal confrontations.

In the next chapter, let's go through some six golden rules to consider when investing in cryptocurrencies.

THE SIX GOLDEN RULES
TO CONSIDER WHEN INVESTING
IN CRYPTOCURRENCIES

Many people still have doubts and unending questions related to investing in cryptocurrencies. They aren't sure of the opportunities available and the risks involved. On the other hand, the prices of cryptocurrencies have remained highly volatile, making it possible for ordinary investors to turn into millionaires, millionaires into billionaires, and equally realize the ugly reverse of downgrading billionaires and millionaires into ordinary people.

The crypto market is moving fast and it's almost becoming practically impossible for anyone to make right judgment on which crypto to invest in and which one to shun. In fact, many investors are simply moving with the flow.

To get an edge when investing in cryptocurrencies, there are a number of essential things you must put into consideration. Taking these factors into account should not only reward you with good profit at the end of your investment horizon, but will equally give you peace of mind in case of an eventuality.

Below are the six golden rules to consider when investing in cryptocurrencies.

1. **Never invest any amount of money you can't let go -** any amount you can't afford to lose! This can never be over emphasized.

2. **Have a solid understanding of that which you are investing in.**

   Whether you are a professional or an amateur, the first step towards making a wise crypto-related investment decision is by understanding the basics of that which you are investing in. Warren Buffet's age old investment advice *'never invest in what you don't understand'* is a priceless gem that you can never close your ears and eyes to.

   Broaden your crypto-related knowledge base. Spend some time going through/monitoring crypto-related news. Find forums and exchanges where you can keep yourself updated on the latest developments in the crypto world.

Read as much as you possibly can on cryptocurrencies. And to kick you off, below are some of the famous crypto-related sites to help you gather relevant news, market information and even price projections:

- CoinMarketCap - Though it provides slightly delayed prices (by nearly ten minutes late), it has a compressive and reliable price coverage of more than 1200 coins. You'll access reliable trade volumes, useful charts and even market cap information.

- CryptoCompare.com - If you want access to a live feed of almost all cryptocurrencies out there, this is where to look at. While it works well for the top cryptos, the information of the other cryptos (those below top 20) can't be relied upon here since they take time to update. For the top cryptos, you'll access all the active exchanges and equally get a chance to compare the prevailing prices. And more significant, you'll get reliable data on proof type and algorithms corresponding to each coin.

- CryptoAnswers.net - They generate unique content touching on crypto news, market information, and ICO news. They equally have a YouTube channel where you can access such content.

- CryptoPanic.com - This site aggregates news focusing solely on cryptos. It collects crypto-related news headlines world over and presents them in some easy to digest column. Using it will help preserve your sanity as you struggle to stay up to date with the unending crypto related news.

- Twitter - Find news, articles or views touching on cryptocurrencies via these poplar crypto-related hash tags #cryptocurrencies, #crypto #cryptocurrency #ICO. You can also search any cryptocurrency you are interested in as a hash tag – i.e. #bitcoin, #Litecoin #Ethereum #EOS, #bitcoincash etc.

- Facebook - Just like twitter, just enter the similar hash tags #cryptocurrencies, #crypto #cryptocurrency #ICO. You can also search any cryptocurrency you are interested in as a hash tag – i.e. #bitcoin, #Litecoin #Ethereum #EOS, #bitcoincash etc.

3. Diversify your investment.

Avoid putting all your eggs in one basket. Cryptocurrency is young, and the market has already proven how highly volatile it is. The challenge of trading in cryptos is their unstable prices. You should therefore invest in them not on a stand-alone basis, but as a very small portion of your diversified portfolio.

4. **The earlier the better.**

The most ideal time to invest in any crypto is during the initial offering. Once the frenzy kicks in (like the one surrounding bitcoin's price), you'll definitely need to exercise lots of caution. But armed with the right information, you can still invest in any cryptocurrency of your choice, at any given time.

5. **Get out when you feel it's safe doing so, whether at a profit or at a loss.**

The worst pain to subject yourself through would be to keep holding your coins even when all signs point to a bleak future. The crypto market is still new, with no known pointers to the true values of most coins. The market is highly volatile with chances of making a profit or loss being 50/50. Always strive to starve your greed for more profits and instead use your commonsense when investing.

6. Exercise safety first, always.

Use proven trustworthy crypto wallet holders such as coinbase to keep your coins. Never trust unproven crypto wallet holders. You definitely not know when that hyena will unmask the sheepskin

CRYPTOCURRENCY AND TAXES – THINGS YOU NEED TO KNOW

Since inception, cryptocurrencies have enjoyed 'free trade' (*anonymous transactions and no taxes*), and given the possibility of the coins staying with us for a good period of time, a number of governments are now stepping in to not only preserve the coins from abuse, but to equally cushion consumers from exploitation.

Bitcoin and related cryptos are feeling the heat as new regulations are slowly being enforced by different governments world over. All signs now point to a new dawn where most governments now want to take a bite off the gains of cryptocurrencies by enforcing relevant laws.

In the US for example, the IRS treats cryptocurrency as a property, meaning there are capital gain implications. Unlike the wider public and crypto users who view the coins as digital currencies, the IRS treats them as property - for purposes of tax. This make the selling, exchange (for cash or for other tokens), and spending of the coins to have capital gain implications.

Nonetheless, the sad truth is that many people are not honest. All they want is a quick way out, and would stop at nothing to realize this. In US where one is expected to report crypto-related transactions to IRS, many US based crypto users don't.

But did you know one creative way of minimizing tax on capital gains is by buying and holding for more than a year? However, given cryptos are highly volatile, it's practically not viable to try buying and holding for more than a year.

It would therefore not take long before we see certain aspects of crypto-related transactions such as mining, trading (including exchange) and spending subjected to taxing.

You should therefore stay properly informed with the right information to help you stay ahead of the game rather than be reactionary in the event that future arrives fast.

Below are some of the reasons why these certain aspects of crypto-related transactions seem tax appealing:

Conversion - Changing a cryptocurrency to any local or foreign currency at a profit creates a table event. Most people do this to generate some capital gain - which is legally taxable.

ICOs - ICOs generate income to both its issuers and beneficiaries. It's therefore a potential candidate for taxing.

Means of payment - Getting paid a salary in crypto, or receiving cryptos as payment for goods/services equals receiving an ordinary income, thus deserve taxing.

Exchange - Exchanging one coin for another or using one coin to purchase another coin generally creates a taxable scenario. Notably, the end result would be capital gains or losses since that exchange process is equated to a sale process.

Trading - Trading generally produces two results; gains or losses. Gains (profits) are without any doubt taxable, while losses may be used to offset gains while reducing tax.

Mining - Mining cryptos generate income to the miners and others in the mining chain. That income (usually rewarded inform of cryptos), is therefore a potential candidate for taxing.

Air dropping - Most beneficiaries of crypto air drops do exchange or sell the coins, thereby generating some capital gain in the process. Being a beneficiary of airdrop is therefore, equated to being a beneficiary of an ordinary income - making it taxable event.

IS IT STILL OK TO INVEST IN CRYPTOCURRENCIES?

You've definitely heard many people referring to cryptos as a gamble, or a financial bubble almost exploding. Many continue to advice against investing in them due to volatile prices and lack of solid legal back up. They view the coins as some form of pyramid scheme that will ultimately not end well.

In the course of writing this book, I again asked five of my other close friends about their general views on cryptocurrencies, and their responses weren't surprising.

First one: *Anyone must be having high tolerance for risk to be excited about investing in cryptocurrencies! It's definitely more risky than gambling!*

Second one: *Right now, cryptos are enjoying highly unstable prices making them far from acting as ideal currencies. As an example, just imagine the thought of selling say your home today for $100,000, only to wake up the next day to find the $100,000 you have in your possession has devalued to say $5,000! Such is the trap those investing in cryptocurrencies will ultimately find themselves in.*

Third One: *Currently, the prices of cryptocurrencies are being fueled by lots of both negative and positive speculations – with frontiers of the good news being holders of the coins, while those propagating bad news being non-holders.*

Fourth One: *Acceptance in Philippines and Japan saw the prices rocket, while a possible ban in China was welcomed* by a dip in price. *Just imagine that instability in one country has the potential to lower the value of all cryptocurrencies across the world! I would definitely never waste my money on any crypto.*

Fifth One: *The outcome of investing in any cryptocurrency at the moment is 50/50. You'll either end up making some good money, or lose it all.*

I must admit the cryptocurrency market has its own unique sets of risks. The best cushion for any crypto investor is therefore to have a solid understanding of the technology behind the crypto you are investing in, and its future potential (implementation).

Use of cryptos is new and revolutionary. The potential of cryptos is enormous! So many opportunities for innovation are open, with many already made possible. Consider the following cases:

- *The start of 2018 saw Western Union and Ripple teaming up to test out Ripple's unique transfer technology. In fact, the numbers of financial institutions that are using, testing, and contemplating use of Ripple's transfer technology are on the rise.*

- *Japanese popular and biggest messaging service provider Chat App was set to announce its expansion into provision of financial services that includes cryptocurrencies, loans, insurance and trading (https://t.co/NC37K38wYS)*

- *In sports, a Turkish amateur football club became the first football club to successfully complete a transfer via bitcoin (http://www.whoateallthepies.tv/transfer_talk/267989/turkish-amateurs-harusnustaspor-become-first-ever-football-club-to-pay-transfer-fee-using-bitcoin.html)*

- *Burger King already launched its own cryptocurrency (Whopper coin) for utilization in customers' reward program.*

- *Microsoft announced their embrace of public blockchains (bitcoin, ethereum and other alter coins) for use in building decentralized identity systems. And to start off, the company was working towards supporting blockchain-based decentralized IDs (DIDs) in their Microsoft's Authenticator app.*

- *LitePay, Inc. set to launch instantaneous Litecoin (LTC) payment infrastructure that seeks to grant businesses the ability to accept payments in Litecoins. Equally, there is accompanying Litecoin debit cards - powered by VISA, making transactions instantaneous and easier than before. And interestingly, since the cryptocurrency space is littered with copy and paste, the LitePay's idea to set up the instantaneous payment infrastructure would not take long before being copied by other cryptos - in bid to keep the confidence of their clients.*

- *Most exchanges are almost being outpaced by not only transactions, but equally by new user registrations, exhibiting an explosion of interest that the masses have on the coins.*

Truth is, the cryptos are here for the long haul. They are definitely going nowhere! The world is slowly embracing the coins - with many countries now opting to design their own and putting in circulation. But remember, if you decide to invest in the coins, then follow the six golden rules already highlighted herein.

WHY MOST GOVERNMENTS FIND IT HARD TO BAN BITCOIN AND RELATED CRYPTOCURRENCIES

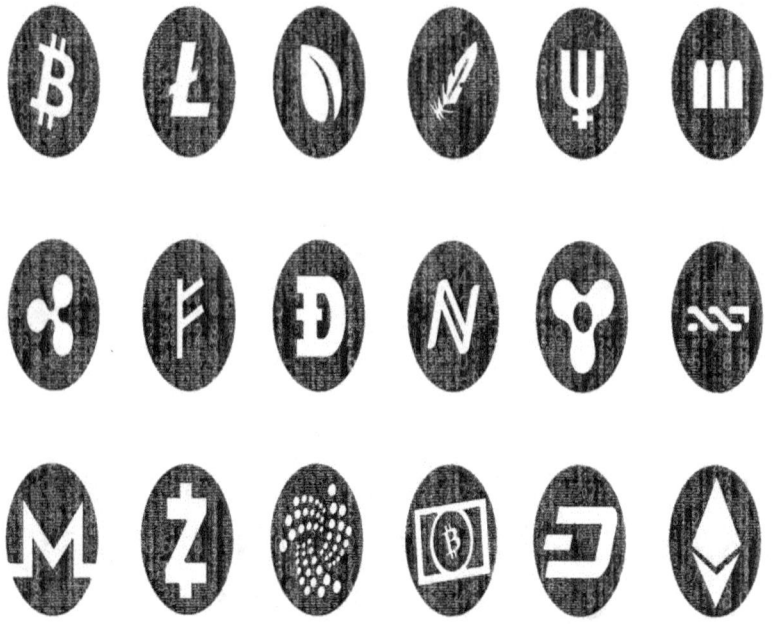

Cryptocurrencies have already provided a benchmark on the direction the future digital money should take, and what most countries that are developing their own digital currencies are engaged in is simply *monkey see monkey do* kind of creations. They still need bitcoin and related cryptocurrencies to help them perfect their various creations.

As at now, many innocent investors already have their hard-earned savings trapped in a number of crypto-related investments. The stakes are very high. Many people are already involved, and a lot of money too is at stake. It would be suicidal trying to totally ban crypto-related dealings.

If bitcoin and co fail, then even most government-backed cryptos will most likely fail too - since many people shall have lost confidence in digital currencies. The success of bitcoin and related cryptocurrencies is therefore key to the success of most government-backed cryptocurrencies.

There are already known shortcomings of bitcoin and related cryptocurrencies such as volatile markets, limited user cases, speculative investments, substandard exchange infrastructures, misleading whitepapers, lack of proper mechanisms to provide redress in situations such as theft etc. However, it won't take long before the various crypto creators start addressing these major shortcomings, eventually solidifying their roles as key players in the crypto space.

Many countries have realized that you can't ban trade in bitcoin and related cryptocurrencies, then go ahead and launch your own cryptocurrency and expect it to be successful. The citizens might end up revenging (by declining to uptake it) thus rendering the project unsuccessful. Bitcoin and co will continue complimenting various government-backed cryptocurrencies and possibly offering better returns - in the near future.

A number of government backed cryptocurrencies are being developed to deal with certain specific local issues such as solving debt crisis, facilitating online payment for government services, raising funds for government projects, etc - unlike cryptos such as bitcoin that offer global solutions such as providing efficient online means of payment for goods and services - even in environments when trust, or lack of it is a problem.

Many cryptocurrencies being developed by various governments are just but improved versions of the already existing ones. Notably, their central focus is to claim ownership, take control of production and circulation, and be able to limit some of the shortcomings of the already existing cryptos - such as being able to track transactions with a view of thwarting any potential abuse. Don't you think it's suicidal banning that which you are coping or that which you are trying to improve on?

Well, in the next chapter, let's go into detail on why most governments have developed sudden interest in developing their own digital currencies.

WHY MANY COUNTRIES ARE RUSHING IN ON CRYPTOCURRENCIES

In late 2017 after the price of bitcoin had surged to over $17,000, there was increased pro-government stance for cryptocurrencies. The potential of cryptocurrencies is so enormous no country wants to be left behind. A number of countries have already created and launched their own, with many in the process, while others have launched commissions or taskforces with an aim of developing their own cryptocurrencies.

Ecuador became the first government to develop a state-run electronic payment system way back in 2015. Other than Ecuador, China, Singapore, Tunisia, and Senegal have also already launched their own digital currencies. Japan, Estonia, Palestine, Sweden and Russia are at advanced stages towards developing their own cryptos (at the time of writing this book).

Given that cryptocurrencies have been operating in unregulated space since inception, many world governments are stepping in to fill what they perceive as necessary security and control gaps. They are also coming in to reap the fruits of the new kid on the block.

Raising Funds

Using the already tested and proven crowd funding potential of cryptos via ICOs, many countries want to develop their own cryptos towards getting funds to finance major projects. Venezuela's crypto, *'Petro'*, was largely created for meeting such an end. Specifically, it was designed to help the country become more financially independent from the sanction-riddled international financial system.

Source of revenue

Many countries want to generate revenues from crypto-related transactions. It's a major reason why they view the need of developing digital currency as a must.

Limit/Track/ abuse of cryptocurrencies

As already noted, a cryptocurrency such as bitcoin gives its users pseudonymity - making it difficult to track any transaction between two parties. This is widely being cited as a possible security threat since it can conveniently be used to finance terrorist or illegal activities. Many countries feel the need to address this gap through provision of their own controlled cryptos, and being able to track all related transactions.

Taking total control

No country wants to be left out of the vital process of producing and circulating their own legal tenders (digital or fiat). They want their various central banks to do what they do best - control production and circulation of currencies. This is vital to help them tell the true number of coins in circulation, unlike bitcoin and related cryptos whose system of production is subject to some mathematical formula, and mode of circulation is decentralized.

Managing prices and related price volatility

Price volatility has negatively impacted the use of bitcoin and related cryptocurrencies. They are no longer used much as a means of exchange, losing one of the core functions of a viable currency.

Most people who own cryptocurrencies such as bitcoin prefer holding the coins rather than spending it - but why would you spend it when its value will be worth more the next hour or the day?

To take charge of the prices and contain price volatility, many governments are working on introducing relevant legislations, reigning on runaway markets, and providing/supporting legitimate and secure currency exchange structures and platforms.

Improving productivity

Given the advance in technology, many people and businesses find it easy to make or receive payments for goods or services digitally. One of the key benefits of doing so is in saving time. And by saving time, productivity is definitely improved. Most governments want to adopt this by introducing use of cryptocurrencies to pay for government services in a bid to offer convenience, save time, and improve productivity.

THE FUTURE OF THE CRYPTOCURRENCY MARKET

Cryptocurrencies have already grown both in value and popularity. They are gaining traction each new day. They will only crash the moment they became worthless, but are they? Given the increased world governments' interest in taxing, regulating, and legalizing the coins, it shows that there is a deeper interest to not let go of the cryptocurrencies.

The market is poised to witness an increase in more government-backed cryptocurrencies. Each country will eventually develop its own digital currency. Apart from gaining income from related transactions, no country would want to miss out on experiencing the unique and triumphant feeling of creating their own digital currency. Equally, it won't take long before witnessing each economic or regional block creating their respective digital currencies.

Potential regulatory deterrents will continue being witnessed as more central banks and local governments continue paying closer attention to cryptocurrencies - largely so as to exercise control, and to be able to extract revenues from related transactions.

In the days, months, and years ahead, the public will enjoy increased access to sufficient relevant crypto-related data and information, enabling them to make the right investment decisions. Access to such vital data and information would also help manage price volatility - by counter-checking the current negative impact speculation plays in controlling prices of the cryptocurrencies.

The future will witness increased user adoption of cryptocurrencies due to the convenience related to holding and using them. As rightly pointed out by Tim Draper, "*In five years, if you try to use fiat currency, they will laugh at you. Bitcoin and other cryptocurrencies will be so relevant... there will be no reason to have the fiat currencies*".

More platforms will embrace cryptocurrencies. The crypto creators will too find more secure ways of linking with other payment technology providers such as Visa and MasterCard to give convenience to their users.

The future will see large-scale investments into cryptocurrencies. New crypto-related products (features and ETFs) and infrastructure will be introduced, making it easier for increased sums of capital to flow into the system. The space will be revamped by entry of increased number of financial and investment institutions. This will resultantly enable the pumping of significant liquidity and other secure public investment vehicles into the cryptocurrency market. Right now, the cryptocurrency market is starved of liquidity due to participation by limited number of institutional investors and a reduced public finance equity - due to the slow wait and see engagement from many individual investors world over.

More corporates (large, medium and small-sized) will issue their own cryptocurrency tokens - We've already witnessed companies such as Telegram and Kodak launching their own cryptocurrency tokens. This trend will continue over the coming years - with such companies seeking to transform and modernize their technologies and other underlying economics.

An increased number of more secure exchange/trading platforms will be witnessed in the not so distant future.

The Initial coin offerings are equally here to stay. The concept of initial coin offerings as a viable means of raising capital for early stage technology companies gained momentum in late 2016, and has proved its worth to date. ICOs have significantly proved to be effective, cheap, and high-speed alternative means of raising venture capital money.

Speculation will never end. It's the fuel that drives the prices of the coins. And the prices of major cryptocurrencies will continue witnessing upward and downward swings. As at now, it's difficult to tell when the prices will eventually self-correct and stabilize.

Parting Shot

The barrage of warnings that the prices of cryptocurrencies could all come crashing down have endlessly been intense. Weirdly, each time pundits have warned the bubble is almost bursting, the prices have gone low for a few days and then risen and surged upwards thereafter.

The future of bitcoin and related cryptocurrencies is largely dependent on you and me. It's the degree of user acceptance that will determine how viable and valuable each cryptocurrency fairs. Nonetheless, for bitcoin and related cryptocurrencies to be the ultimate future money, they have to compete against the already established payment methods such as fiat money, credit cards, checks, etc.... and come top in the race.....And yes, they have slowly started to overtake these established payment methods!

Bitcoin and related cryptocurrencies have surged from fringe investments to global sensations. A clear takeaway is: they are here to stay. They've definitely crafted a path that is bound to change the future of global financial systems.

And the recovery of the markets and the rebounding of the prices of the major cryptocurrencies to their all time high is always never too far away!

THE END